Split-Level

poems by

D. R. James

Finishing Line Press
Georgetown, Kentucky

Split-Level

for
Danny, Derek, Peter, and Michael
and for Suzy

ACKNOWLEDGMENTS

Caring Magazine: "Hospice Report"
Coe Review: "Teaching" and "Upgrade"
The Curator: "Country Crow"
Eclectica: "A Theology"
The Mas Tequila Review: "Trying to Write My Way Out of This Paper Bag" and
"EKG Whiz"
Old Northwest Review: "Rite of Passage"
Pudding Magazine: "Inter-Faith Dialogue"
Spilt Infinitive: "Hospice Report"
Talking River: "Ash Wednesday," "Hornets," "Maybe They're Brothers," and "Split-
Level"
The Tower Journal: "10-4-80," "Percussion," "Trying to Write about My Youngest
Son," and "With Less Than a Year to Live My Mother Reveals She Was Friends
with The Fugitive"
Town Creek Poetry: "True North"

Publisher: Leah Maines

Editor: Christen Kincaid

Cover Art: Meridith Ridl

Author Photo: Susan James

Cover Design: Elizabeth Maines

Printed in the USA on acid-free paper.
Order online: www.finishinglinepress.com
also available on amazon.com

Author inquiries and mail orders:
Finishing Line Press
P. O. Box 1626
Georgetown, Kentucky 40324
U. S. A.

Table of Contents

I.

Split-Level

When my parents built us a faux-colonial
they demanded the stairwell be shifted
off-center to prevent visitors from peering
straight up at someone in the bathroom.

Dad said those rubes carving allotments
out of cornfields a "day's wagon ride"
west of Chicago that first year into
Kennedy's presidency had to be told

to use round-nosed white oak trim
on the stair treads, tongue-and-groove
hardwood up as well as down, and to
angle the single overheads out the side

so the garage's twin windows hung
with Mom's tie-back curtains would
simulate a 'wing' from the street.
Everyone else moving in for the boom

was building split-levels, whose two sets
of stubby half-stairs eliminated basements,
one floor only half underground, the other
half again above the lawn. The locals

had settled in their tiny '20's bungalows
around the quaint downtown—their names
labeling diner, dry cleaner, five-and-dime—
or out on dwindling farms, so long entrenched

they had to double-check not to date
their cousins. Coming in from Cleveland,
I didn't know I'd never fit. Not from town,
not from the country, not in line with the

subdivided life, I didn't know I'd wander
to someplace inside, somewhere below grade.
In bed summer nights, screened windows
propped wide, I'd listen to the new Japanese

motorcycles whining the humid half-miles
stop sign to stop sign, immense mosquitoes
flying right by, flying away along the asphalt
corridors gridding corn and soy beans as I lay

stuck to my sheets in the daylight-saving dusk,
wondering what to make of my own backyard.

Rite of Passage

In Bali, it's the filing of the canines
to limit boys' wild adolescence.
Among Cameroon's Baka Pygmies
it's the Spirit of the Forest killing

boys to be reborn as men. And in rural
Illinois, 1964, the May grass brilliant,
resilient as Astro Turf, it's initiation
for the fraternity of boys-who-mow.

My turn now to untangle the Craftsman
from the rakes and bikes, top it off
with the dregs of last year's gasoline,
find my chest exceeds the handles,

but I can barely pull the cord. It takes
twenty tugs, more and less throttle,
more and less choke, for the engine
to catch, cough, and wreathe me in its

blue-black smoke. Then maneuvering
the sidewalk is easy, dried leaves
and spring debris parting as I push.
But once I clear the pavement, bounce

down into that first of countless rounds,
I become a summer Sisyphus, mini-
supplicant leaning into the pleasure
of some sadistic god. Luckily it's

post-Ike, post-JFK, so the power-push
is soon supplanted by the self-propelled
and the Wheel Horse rider. Slow-forward
eight years, parents away on vacation,

and I take to trick-driving in third gear,
careening in circles, graduate at my
County job to Farmall tractors, tires
taller than fence posts, Brush Hogs whose

twin two-foot blades mangle anything
along a country road. One breezy day
in May, I find where Midwest rabbits nest—
in the green shade of a fencerow crabapple,

invisible amidst the long grass eight feet in
from the shoulder. And once I've run
the lowered mower over them, glanced
back to see a dozen brown and blue-red

bodies roiling behind the roar, I mimic
how other men can keep on mowing.

Maybe They're Brothers

these two, slow-riding
a clown-tiny bicycle
up my gradual hill, one,

slightly larger, pedaling,
swaying over the seat,
the other, lock-kneed

astride the rear tire, feet
fixed to steel axle pegs,
his two hands holding

the bigger boy's hips above
the pistons of his thighs.
Meanwhile, their happy

chatter, which I can hear
but not quite make out,
goes on nonstop even when

the pedaler's left slip-on
slips off and the passenger,
touching down on the run,

retrieves and positions it
to slip back on. Seamless,
like a two-man bob-sled

crew, except to resume
an ascent, they regroup
and push off, wobbly

then steady as before, and
vanish around the corner
toward the convenience store.

Or maybe they're best friends,
like Jimmy and me, in '63, him
pedaling, me hanging on.

10 – 4 – 80
—for Danny
—after Roland Flint

Well, Danny, tomorrow morning
you will be born—if this were 36
years ago, and I were 26.

Twenty-six! How young I'd be
even to you now, first son!
A mere boy. *Was* I still

a boy at 26—seeing my
first baby—my first before
three more—seeing you?

If I'm thinking of you more,
am I getting ready to be reborn
myself or do I miss you

from reading a fellow poet
who puts an aching
spin on living close,

the way we did for so long,
almost eighteen years
before divorce closed down

the life we lived together,
the mundane comings
and goings that didn't

register enough all through?
Remember? I do, and I'll
remember them to you:

how you waited twenty
hours to emerge, your angst
in any candy store, *which*

sport to go pro in, how your
wobbly ankles grew into
the quickest on the field,

your mind the most litigious
in your class, your tears the fiercest
when you heard our news.

Percussion
—for Derek

All summer I shadow your band
from the porch: London to Rome,
Lausanne to Amsterdam,
a week on Sardinia, then back

to Liverpool, Mecca of my youth.
And besides my usual obsessions—
your precarious health, the requisite
excesses—I worry about

each venue's resident drum kit—
whether there are two toms, a kick-drum,
high-hat, ride and crash cymbals,
a decent snare—and whether

the bale of the bucket,
the turquoise floor-mop bucket,
the one your older brother
rigged up for you

from the laundry room
to be your bright bass drum,
will still slip easily
over your head and your

Dutch-boy bangs
to lead the parade
of neighbor kids, kazoos,
garbage-lid cymbals,

up one side of Fourteenth Street
and down the other, forever
marching, forever playing
my arrhythmic heart

back here in Holland,
Michigan.

Hornets
—for Peter
—after James McKean

You were coveting
the other side of the creek
and the sun-streaked dune and the trees
sand-propped up the slope
but missed the hornets
in their late-summer nest, holed-up
at log's end as you crossed,
your toy grappling gear shoulder-slung.
When you looked back
I was grateful again
that such weekends camouflaged the failures
of divorce. We were family—
one dad, two youngest sons, this chance
to play together and
we could choose, your brother, you, and I, how
much to make of it,
bare-footed and lazy
the length of those daylight-saving days.
What languid resistance!
But above the combs your foot broke through,
chuting your pant leg
into that awful upward swarm
toward which your split-second expression, empty-eyed,
and panicked, I regret,
refocused me, penitent dreamer,
intermittent vigilant,
who hears his son's agony echoing
and sees his son's terror replayed
second by second through this blue
afternoon.

Trying to Write about My Youngest Son
—for Michael

It doesn't help when—my eyes
closed, head tilted back
to picture you more distinctly

as the second tallest now
among your three adult brothers—
you come strutting again

through the preschool's double-doors,
serious as a police commissioner,
the tail on your tissue-paper kite

zigging the tulip-lined sidewalk
behind you, your face all
bouncing cheeks, perfect, pouting lips.

Or that when I manage to capture
your *chiseled* jaw and shoulders
but can't come up with a better word

you barrel back from Ann Arbor
in your Cherokee, and *chiseled*
is still the only word. This spree

from tee-ball to a degree
in engineering—
what your grandfather, my father,

and your great-grandfather
mastered before you—what your
beautiful mathematical mind

has finally decided for you—
compresses within me
as if the squeezebox of my years

were in full exhale, my hands
pressed together around it
like a little boy's, in prayer.

Upgrade

"Oh, man, that flip-phone's toast!" coughs
the sales dude at the iStore in the outlet mall
before muscling me into an upgrade
A. G. Bell himself would've called
bullshit on. With a switchblade on a
bracelet he slits the copper wrapper
of a smartphone that will render me
dumb again—my thimbleful of techno-
info a nemesis that throws each round—

and fires it up. Meanwhile, I zoom
to old BU, where Watson's sipping soup
just as Bell elbows the acid that prompts his
iconic yelp. Three-piece tweeds—ready-made
or the tailored upgrade—make the brightest
prone to spilling—and as I'm considering
switching from my flannels and dungarees
the iDude flags me back from Boston: "Mr.
Dimson...come here...I want to fleece you."

Country Crow

When cars approach at ten over, ten under,
I think: stay with the carrion at this edible
consistency or do my flap-away-and-wait?

The zoom is monotonous, all buzz and swoosh,
a rhythm I live with, my murder and me.
And I've heard we're confused for starlings,

for grackles, though how? No speckles. No
iridescent heads. We're bigger, more mythical.
Some say majestic! Maybe. From a distance.

But on the fat branch of this fencerow mulberry
it's merely watch and wait. Some dull days
I never stretch my wings, just hop from crotch

to pavement and back again, and back again,
a little bluish viscera dangling from my beak.
You'd never know it but the hawk's no bigger,

though the search light of his shadow casting
wide circles over roadways, over fields means
he'll soon have live meat. Me, I get what

gets itself hit. Then in between I doze and dream
I'm small enough to ride a bowing cattail.
Slurring a scratchy *terrr-eee*, an *oak-a-lee*,

flashing my red and yellow chevrons
luminescent in the summer sun,
I'm catching someone's eye.

II.

Writing My Way out of this Paper Bag

is a lot like unlocking
Pandora's box (which was actually
an urn, πίθος, I looked it up)
if it'd been a shoe box, the hefty,
faux-hemp-textured kind with a hinged top
and rounded side flaps, pride-and-joy
of a junior packaging engineer (of which there
really are such positions, *starting* at $67K, I've asked),
only when it's flung open, as if to allow
all hell to break loose, it reveals
wads of beige tissue paper, an anti-
moisture packet shaped like a gauzy ravioli
without the sauce, and a glossy
brochure on pursuing life as an adventure,
(sporting their 'gear,' of course) that somebody
had to write and nobody ever reads,
but me. This Pandora's box
that's like the bag out of which
I'm writing my way
just sits here like I left it
when I laced up the water-proof boots,
retro-fitted with my orthotics, and wore them
over sweat-wicking socks to the office
to grade papers and bitch about the dean.
And any diseases or plagues or other
acts of gods (unclear in the Greek, unlike
in the O. T., I checked),
whose disgorging from the horrid box
I might have artfully bemoaned,
simply fizzle,
just like this petty pitter-patter,
and I'm left with an albeit manly box
that I probably should recycle. Or

it's like having set out to see a certain big city
for the first time—say, Mumbai, a.k.a. Bombay—
with the intention of having the experience
hit me like an aesthetic ton of bricks
(only I'd come up with a better comparison),
but due to some predictable drizzle,
maybe a monsoon, or more likely
lack of funds (since I drop a dozen hundred
rupees every time I open my billfold)
and/or a fear of big cities (this one
in particular, it turns out),
I sit in my mid-price, fourth-floor hotel room
in cargo shorts and a T-shirt that reads,
"What would Prufrock do?" and watch
a *Mannix* marathon with Marathi subtitles
because it reminds me of the guys in high school
and how Mrs. Wolf marked all the creative punctuation
wrong in my ninth–grade poetry portfolio,
something Mike Connors wouldn't have stood for
if he'd ever written poetry. Or

like when I have a breakthrough in analysis
after weeks of getting this latest therapist up to speed
and then, by the time I pull into the driveway,
I forget the key phrase he gave me—
something about the pre-frontal capacity
for being of two minds. Or

like in the dream where I'm trying to two-thumb a text
to my twenty-four year old (only
when he was five), but multiple
in-comings from a life-insurance salesman
keep sending it to *Drafts.* Or

it's like accepting a challenge
to write my way out of a paper bag
only to discover it's too dark inside,
and besides, it has a waxy finish,
so my pen won't go.

Teaching
—after Richard Jones

Then, it was easy to believe
the gentle world
to be sad. Rereading
for class, feeling
the old and scribbling
a few new remarks
in the margins
of thick anthologies, heavy
as brick—(denying Pope
his idiotic confidence
in the trustful licking
of a gamboling lamb;
seconding Ivan Ilyich
in all his too-late
second-guessings, the
light he could only see
at the bottom
of his suffocating sack;
or granting Beckett's
every twisted take,
those mad clowns marooned
at the dead ends
of their imaginations)—
I'd think of my students,
strolling across campus
in their innocence
to my classroom,
where, for fifty minutes,
I'd rant and they'd maybe
consider the many things
that couldn't make us happy.

Hospice Report
—for Suzy

My wife comes home, cold, slides
into bed to warm against my sleepiness,

and sighs. *That snow. I drove
through everything.* To the toddler

who never walked, and every Friday
for eighteen months beyond predictions,

his slack presence swaddled on the
living room couch. Encephalitis—

nothing wrong with that little heart.
Though the tiny mother's had broken

long ago, and now her nonstop sobbing,
her husband posted like friendly stone,

the older brothers already back in bed.
She'd held him dead for two hours

before the nurse could carry him outside.
How are *you* I whisper, my wife's body

beginning to settle. *Always sad for them,
but happy for the baby,* who was too big

for the funeral man's basket, small enough
to stow beside him on the seat.

With Less Than a Year to Live My Mother Reveals
She Was Friends with *The Fugitive*

"Oh, he was a handsome fella—but a bum." We're
in her mini living room, Dad two years dead,
her foot twitching like she's on to something
and knows how to get us. Something juicy.

"Could've played for Ohio State, I guess," but
wanted to be a doctor like his dad. "Dr. Sheppard!"
As kids they'd spy on his brother with girlfriends,
"Lots of those around," before Sam became a BMOC

himself: A-student, class president, "ladies' man"
at Cleveland Heights High. I say I can't believe
she hasn't told us all this before. "You never asked,"
she says and starts to reel us in: "I didn't know Marilyn

until after they married. She seemed nice enough."
Nobody ever knew if she knew he fooled around.
"When they moved out our way—I'd just had you—
I couldn't figure which lakeshore drive was theirs."

Until the murder later made it a crime scene. He
blamed a bushy-haired man. Nobody believed him.
Ten years later, F. Lee Bailey got him acquitted,
"so maybe there was. But did you realize

he went into pro wrestling? Yeah!" *The Killer*
with the *mandible claw*. She taps her foot, gazes
out the bay window toward the courtyard and gazebo,
says, "I've always felt bad I never welcomed her."

EKG Whiz

Thump, thump,
Old Ticker!

Well, older
than I thought—
little red flag
needling upside
my neck. *Yawn...*

and the race
was on. I
picture that tube
that scope thin
as a micro-
scopic snake,

its headlight
nosing: 3 trickles
to discover, 3
to open up,
widen the criks
to irrigate
the whole
unbought farm,

chicken wire
to hold back
them nasty
water weeds,
to stent
me growth.

Thump, thump,
Old Ticker!

A Theology

Until this morning, infinity
had never listened. My heart,
which nearly died five years ago,
the blood slacking
gradually but surely

in the geography
of my brief body,
always hesitated to hear
what alone held it
in time's bald gaze.

Then, this morning, four a.m.,
a bird, his *Ee-oo, oo-Eh*
echoing off brick, unanswered
over Pacific Avenue,
taught my heart to listen.

Ash Wednesday

This life of separateness may be compared to a dream, a phantasm,
a bubble, a shadow, a drop of dew, a flash of lightning. —*The Buddha*

The heat kicking in at precisely five a.m.
stirs the shirred glass chimes dangling over
the open vent, their fragile song reminding me
I am alone. Outside, where I know too-early

browns loom in the dark where constant white
should lighten this time of year—here, far
north of the end of Mardi Gras—one car
purrs by per hour. A semi ascending the hill,

up-shifting its dissonance across the cushion
of the dumb neighborhood, will turn left
at the next intersection, head east to open road,
and merge with the world. This separateness

is indeed a dream, though priests today will call
the many to mourn whatever separates them
from God and from each other, then swipe soaked
ash across their foreheads in remembrance that

we're all just dust. Which is true, but in this
blue mood I prefer the Buddha's drop of dew
and picture its sole self temporarily resting
upon a palm leaf before a breeze shivers it

earthward or the desert sun draws it skyward—
in either case to mingle it by absorption
or by evaporation into the eternal system
of one. Which is really only a better way

of getting it wrong. Poor sentient drop, alive
in the thought it has ever left its sisters and brothers,
who in their own dreams manufacture fantastic
bubbles but imagine wry shadow, or lightning.

Inter-Faith Dialogue

Jesus was a Capricorn.
—Kris Kristofferson

And a plagiarist. Pilfered
his material sometime
after the temple—
Mary and Joseph crazy
till they found him, beardless
among the beards—
and before the Jordan—
Cousin John still with his head
if not his right mind. Jesus
hung up the leather vest
of right livelihood,
dropped his dad's hammer
onto the olive wood table,
hitched a caravan to Sarnath
and became a Buddhist.

In the neighborhood he'd made
people nervous, always looking
right into them, his primal
right mindfulness awkward
at parties. But now Gautama's
hard-earned dharma
with an Aramaic spin might
do the trick, might play well
on that mount outside town.

And it did. Until it didn't.
Noble Truth Two became the ones
about the ravens and sparrows.
Right intention: thou shalt not even kill
with the vague hate in thy heart.
And his emptiness? Could've inspired
the Heart Sutra himself: "He has not
been made to tremble, has overcome
what can upset." Rabbi, Bodhisattva—
six of one, half a dozen the other.
Son of God. Son of Man.
Had his own *Dhammapada*.

When the soldiers showed up,
all hell didn't break loose.
That came later. Instead,
the healed ear of right action.
The right speech of saying
nothing at all. Lotus lily
of Kusinagara, of
Skull Hill.

True North

The lone crow on the lone pole
where the weathervane used to whirl
insinuates my need for misdirection.

He is an arrow of skittish attention,
of scant intention: the cock and hop,
the flick and caw toward anything

on the wind. Now angling east, now
south by southwest, he designates
with beak then disagreeing tail feathers,

with a lean-to and a shoulder scrunch,
with an attitude from his beady black eye—
as if he were ever the one to judge.

And once he's spun like a pin on a binnacle
past all points of some madcap inner compass—
once the clouds have bowed to push on

and the grasses waved their gratefulness—
he unfurls the shifty sails of his wings
and the breeze relieves him of his post.

D. R. JAMES is the author of the poetry collection *Since Everything Is All I've Got* (March Street 2011) and four previous poetry chapbooks, including *Why War* (Finishing Line 2014). Poems have appeared in many print and online magazines as well as the anthologies *Poetry in Michigan/Michigan in Poetry* (New Issues 2013) and *Ritual to Read Together: Poems in Conversation with William Stafford* (Woodley 2013). He lives in Saugatuck, Michigan, with his wife, hospice bereavement counselor and cycling partner Susan Doyle, and together they have six children and three grandchildren. James earned his M.A. in English at the University of Iowa and his MFA in poetry at Pacific University and has been teaching writing, literature, and peace-making at Hope College for thirty-two years. Otherwise, he divides his time between looking at the woods from his recliner and looking at the woods from his deck.

CPSIA information can be obtained
at www.ICGtesting.com
Printed in the USA
LVOW12s0408190117

521501LV00001B/12/P